# The Candle and Her Wick

Stephanie Jimenez

BookLeaf
Publishing

Presentation by *BookLeaf Publishing*

Web: www.bookleafpub.com

E-mail: info@bookleafpub.com

ISBN: 9789357617635

First edition 2023

*This book is dedicated to you: the reader. May you find comfort in these pages.*

*I would also like to dedicate this book to my family and good friends. You are my everything.*

*For my mom: I do not have enough time in this lifetime to be able to properly repay you for your love, patience, sacrifice, and dedication. Thank you for teaching me to believe in my dreams and for being our compass.*

*For the person who first showed me the magic behind a good hug and having a best friend. She also taught me how to spell the word friend: My big sister. I love you and please do not spell-check my book.*

*This is also for my niece and nephew and their great example of a dad: my brother. May you always have the courage to believe in yourselves and follow your dreams. You are my inspiration.*

*Last but not least, I would like to dedicate this book to my partner in love and life: my husband. Thank you for believing in me and for teaching me to love and believe in myself. Daring to dream is not so scary with you by my side. You are my greatest adventure.*

# The Candle and Her Wick

There: they are one, the candle and her wick.
A flickering dance, they work together.
To not see this you would have to be thick.
A perfect match, no matter the weather.

Her wick never ceases to light her smile.
In darkness this light shines bright like a star.
As one, they wear resilience with style.
Their love is so pure, some find it bizarre.

Together: a warm, everlasting flame.
In light and darkness, sunrise and sunset.
When they locked eyes their love was set
aflame.
Their laughter and smiles are a small subset.

A smaller element of their grand love.
So perfectly made, it fits like a glove.

# Flower Child

There she is effortlessly beautiful:
with a book, under the sky and the trees.
No one expects her to be dutiful
laying there alone with her memories.

Painting the day with her father the sun,
dancing at night with her mother the moon,
healing with nature creating much fun,
It's life's recipe, it cures every wound.

Her friend the rain washes away her tears.
Fears disappear as she weathers the storm.
Sweet singing birds bring a smile to her ears.
Now peace, love, and joy have all been reborn.

Thank you for washing away all the pain.
Thank you to the moon, the sun and the rain.

# Monsters and Magic

Believe with your heart that you are enough.
Pay no matter to what they have to say.
You are a precious diamond in the rough.
Yes, eventually monsters go away.

They grit their teeth and point their claws at you.
Screeching judgment and striking with their lies.
They must not know who they are talking to.
You will rise, they are in for a surprise.

Win the fight: being true to who you are.
Don't let them win, don't let them see you cry.
Keep rising up. Leave their judgment afar.
Please believe this: It matters when you try.

Your heart and brain and soul are pure magic.
Not seeing that would be truly tragic.

# Trickery

Your inner critic is truly a witch.
Not the good kind with bright healing powers.
Do not believe her and go flip the switch.
She hides the lever in the top tower.

Her spells have been cast so that you can't see.
How valuable and powerful you are.
Your brain is worth more than any degree.
Your wisdom and love will take you so far.

Use your white magic. Put her in her place.
Her insecurities and grief you'll beat:
Using forgiveness, and most of all grace.
Your self-love is the ultimate defeat.

Look out, do not fall for her trickery.
Now nothing can stop you from victory.

# Feel to Heal

Sometimes joy, sometimes grief: let yourself
feel.
An emotional state or reaction.
No matter what it reveals, you can heal.
Action is what can bring satisfaction.

Taking action is making a brave choice.
I promise it will be worth it to make:
A choice to express and respect your voice.
This will bring healing that no snake can take.

Now close your eyes and listen to your heart.
Feel your feelings, no matter what they are.
Yes, opening up is the hardest part.
It's also step one to heal your heart's scar.

Feel your feelings and make them your best
friend.
Believe it will be worth it in the end.

# The Great Pretender

Why are we so afraid of feeling fear?
Avoiding it at all costs: now bankrupt.
We close our eyes and hope it disappears.
But there it remains, abrupt and corrupt.

A thief in the night: stealing hopes and dreams.
Pretending to protect while it destroys.
Take time to see: Fear is not what it seems.
It fills up your head, but it is just noise.

Turn up the volume on love and courage.
Flip the off switch of insecurities.
Now you will see that fear feels discouraged.
No longer feeding off impurities.

Please believe you are anything but small.
You are perfectly made with flaws and all.

# Front Page News

My friend, I need to tell you a secret.
I am beyond elated to share this.
It's kind of big and you won't believe it.
Please promise that its truth you won't dismiss.

You see, it's quite a big discovery.
This really should be on the front page news.
It's shocking. You might need recovery.
Yes, even if there are so many clues.

This secret that I have to share with you…
Is something that you really need to know.
I think it might keep you from being blue.
It can warm your heart when you're feeling low.

The secret's not so secret, but it's true.
It's that you are incredible. Yes, you.

# Return to Sender

That inkling of doubt might creep right in.
Telling you: You can't and won't and didn't!
Lingering, it takes your head for a spin.
Telling you to give up and take a hint.

Don't listen. Not even a little bit.
Your hopes and dreams are worth much more
than that.
You have too much heart in your art to quit.
Love. That's all you need to win this combat.

Love what you do and love how you do it.
Love where it takes you and love why you care.
Love it more than you would ever admit.
Love it like a teen playing truth or dare.

So, send your doubt packing. Send it away.
All that matters is what YOU have to say.

# Dear Inner Children

You are truly perfect just as you are.
I hope you can see that you are a gem.
Your light shines so bright, like a golden star.
You can succeed, in the arts, or in STEM.

So take a deep breath and just be yourself.
Today you can dance or play in the sand.
Tomorrow you'll read a book off the shelf.
As long as you like what you do: it's grand!

Please take note that you are not what you do.
Enjoy it and learn, continue to grow.
You don't have to let one thing define you.
Always let your imagination flow.

There's only one you, so wonderfully made.
Wow, you're so special. Let's have a parade!

# Long Lost Love

I'll always love you. That's what I told you.
Some might not believe that this still holds true.
Ever after was not on the menu.
Especially when the resentment grew.

You went from "the one" to "we were too
young."
Now you turned into lessons I learned.
You know, in the end, I think we both won.
I think our present has had that confirmed.

At my darkest hour you were my friend.
And for this I will always be grateful.
Believe me, I do not mean to offend.
Crossing paths was undoubtedly fateful.

I wish you healing and truly the best.
Nothing but grace and love on your next quest.

# Earth Angel

I met an earth angel just passing by.
Full of love and joy all shared with his smile.
I miss you. I'll never understand why…
Your time with us lasted such a short while.

Your laughter and hugs, such comforting
warmth.
Someone like you, I'll never meet again.
After you left it was hard to go forth.
My sanity, I worked hard to regain.

I'll always feel proud of who you once were.
And often I'll wonder who you are now.
Saying goodbye…wish it did not occur.
But I know we will meet again somehow.

Heaven called you back: Angel, you are missed.
We were so lucky to see you exist.

# Checkmate

I have been playing chess with a stranger.
As familiar strangers, we compete.
Sometimes I feel like I am in danger…
With the lengths, she will go to have me beat.

It's a long game, we have not reached
checkmate.
Though she's gotten close, I always catch on.
She's pretty quick too, she won't take the bait.
Though recently I learned she is a con.

She has been pretending to have power.
But she is just a ghost. The ghost of me…
Haunting and trying to overpower.
She is a shadow; she is the past me.

It's been a long game. I finally won.
Never again haunted by anyone.

# The Sky Is Falling

When you feel like the sky is falling down...
And it feels like everything is spinning
It's okay to frown but don't drop your crown.
Just think: every end is a beginning.

It is okay to feel scared, change is hard.
But harder than change is no change at all.
No, don't treat your feelings with disregard.
You're a human being, not a ragged doll.

It's okay to sigh. Do it heavily.
It's okay to stomp your feet and cry out.
Be kind to yourself, your heart feels heavy.
Do what feels better. Go ahead and shout.

Do what you need to do to feel better.
Then remember that you're a go-getter.

# Day by Day

Tell me: What is your favorite kind of day?
What makes your smile brighter and happy?
Is it a rainy day? A sunny day?
A joyful day that some might call sappy?

Who cares what they think as long as you smile?
Do it for yourself and do what you like.
It's your turn to rest, dance, and stay a while.
You can read a book and then ride your bike.

Whatever it is that gives you freedom...
Alone or in company day by day
And if they won't come then you don't need
them.
It makes YOU happy so: Hip hip hooray!

Make sure that you live a life worth living.
One that is for you, truly, free-living.

# 'Tis the Season

Yes, sharing is kind and kindness is nice.
But this life is not just for serving them.
You have to be careful. Don't roll the dice.
Your time is precious for you and for them.

Do not take it for granted. Not one bit.
Make sure you understand, practice and live.
Sometimes you will forget but just don't quit.
Please don't. Even when life gets aggressive.

Not everything happens for a reason.
It just happens. Action, no reaction.
Like leaves and snow falling. 'Tis the season.
It is a natural interaction.

Love is the greatest gift you can send.
Life is beautiful and so are YOU, friend.

# Smiling Star

Glittering brightly...
A beautiful baby star.
Your smile warms my heart.

# Little Bean

17

How can something small...
Be as big as life itself?
Changing everything.

# Accidentally on Purpose

Happy Accident...
Accidentally in love.
It feels meant to be.

# It's Magic

19

I once met magic.
She looked and smiled at me.
That was just the start.

# Book Butterfly

You hide in your book?
Stay as long as you would like.
Yes, you are safe here.

# Dear Reader

21

Every single page-
Was written with love for you.
I hope you liked it.

Printed in the USA
CPSIA information can be obtained
at www.ICGtesting.com
CBHW071031270924
14863CB00140B/1278